21 MIRACLE *Testimonies*™

by

Rochelle Johnson-Wiggins

ISBN: 979-8-9954212-4-5

Printed in the United States of America.

This book is a faith-based collection of personal testimonies intended to inspire hope, healing, and spiritual reflection.

ACKNOWLEDGEMENTS

First and foremost, I give thanks to God, the ultimate Author and Sustainer of my life. Without His grace, guidance, and unwavering love, this book would not have been possible. His miracles, both seen and unseen, have inspired every word within these pages.

A heartfelt thank you to my husband, Ricky Wiggins, for your steadfast love, encouragement, and unwavering support. Your belief in me and in this vision made all the difference. I am truly blessed to walk this journey with you by my side.

To my children, grandchildren, godchildren, my sister Kelliejay, family, and friends: thank you for your prayers, encouragement, and understanding. Your faith in me kept me going, even on the days when the path felt uncertain. Every word of support and every act of kindness helped to carry me forward.

I am deeply grateful to my editor, Nakia Dorsey, of *I-Am-It's-A-Movement*. Your wisdom, patience, and sharp editorial insight helped shape this manuscript into something clear, powerful, and heartfelt. Thank you for believing in this project and walking with me through every revision.

I also extend my sincere appreciation to Dr. Denise Wilkins for designing the cover of this book. Your creativity, vision, and attention to detail beautifully captured the heart and message of these testimonies, and your work added depth, excellence, and visual impact to this project.

These testimonies come from real-life experiences. I share them with the hope that they reveal the extraordinary ways God works in ordinary lives, and that they remind you that miracles are alive, active, and available.

With all my heart,

Rochelle Johnson-Wiggins

TABLE OF CONTENTS

TESTIMONY 1

The Miracle of Revelation – From Day to Night

When Heaven Spoke Through the Storm: A Grandmother's Faith, a Child's Awakening, and the God Who Makes Himself Known

There are moments in life when something simple, like a voice, a memory, or even a storm, becomes a doorway to something divine.

For me, that doorway often came through the quiet strength of my grandmother. She shared her faith in subtle but powerful ways that lingered long after the moment had passed. On stormy days, she would still the room with her voice and say, "Hush, child! God is speaking." I didn't fully understand the weight of her words then, but they settled in my spirit like seeds, waiting for their time to bloom.

She also introduced me to religious films that made the Bible feel alive and close. The two that left a lasting impression were *Jesus of Nazareth* and *The Ten Commandments.* I was especially moved by *Jesus of Nazareth*, its depiction of Jesus's compassion, His miracles, and the heart-wrenching scenes of His crucifixion which stirred something deep in me. The stories I had only heard in bits and pieces were now unfolding before my eyes with color, emotion, and meaning. They didn't just tell me who Jesus was, they helped me feel Him. These films quietly nurtured my spiritual curiosity, planting truths that would later come to life in the most unexpected way.

One particular day, after watching *Jesus of Nazareth*, I found myself reflecting on a conversation I'd once had with my grandmother. She had spoken of a time when night and day would become indistinguishable. I hadn't understood her words then, but that was about to change.

Later that afternoon, while I was outside, a sudden and violent storm rolled through the skies of Ohio. The sky darkened as thunder rumbled with a voice-like authority, lightning tore across the sky, and rain poured in torrents. What had been a bright, sunny day quickly turned into deep, unsettling darkness.

In that moment, something shifted inside me. I wasn't just witnessing a storm; I was witnessing a revelation. The stories and Scriptures I had been shown came alive before my eyes. I remembered my grandmother's voice: "God is speaking." And this time, I believed it. The storm became more than just weather; it became a divine encounter. I felt God's presence, not distant or abstract, but near, powerful, and real. I wasn't afraid. I was in awe. And all I could whisper was, "WOW, there is a God!" And in that moment, I knew this was a miracle.

"I must work the works of him that sent me, while it is day: the night cometh, when no man can work."

— John 9:4 (KJV)

"And it shall come to pass in that day, saith the Lord GOD, that I will cause the sun to go down at noon, and I will darken the earth in the clear day."

— Amos 8:9 (KJV)

Worship Reflection: *"It's Gonna Rain"* – Reverend Milton Brunson

That day was my first true encounter with the living Word. For the first time, Scripture was not just something I heard or read; it was something I experienced. The divine felt personal. God was not confined to the pages of a book or the scenes of a film. He was present in my life, moving through the world in ways I could feel and witness.

It was a profound realization: God speaks. He moves. And sometimes, He uses even the storms to draw us closer.

TESTIMONY 2

Through the Fire: A Childhood Mistake, a Mother's Love, and the Miracle of God's Protection

Some moments stay with you forever, not because you want them to, but because they change something deep inside you.

I was just a child, doing something as simple as trying to make a grilled cheese sandwich, when my life was nearly turned upside down in an instant. What happened next could have ended in tragedy, but by the grace of God, it became a testimony of His protection over my life.

I recall a frightening experience involving a gas stove and a grilled cheese sandwich. I had tried to light the pilot light myself, as was sometimes necessary with older models. But instead of a small, manageable flame, a sudden burst of fire flared up, much larger than I had anticipated. Startled and panicked, I dropped the match and backed away, not realizing that I had just sparked a dangerous fire.

The flame grew quickly. For a moment, I was frozen in fear. I didn't know what to do, and the situation escalated fast. In a panic, I ran outside, shouting, "Help! Help! There's a fire!" Everything after that is a blur. I must have blacked out for a moment because the next thing I remember, I was surrounded by a neighbor and what looked like the entire Cleveland Fire Department. Their quick response prevented what could have been a devastating tragedy.

While I am incredibly grateful for my safety, I can't help but reflect on the extraordinary circumstances that led to my escape. It felt like more than just good luck, it felt like divine intervention. I'm still processing the impact this experience has had on me. I walked away unharmed, and that alone is something I will never take for granted. I truly believe God had His hand on me that day.

I vividly remember the aftermath: being featured on the local news, the comforting words of Mr. Barnes, a councilman from Cleveland, Ohio, who held me in his arms as he spoke, and the overwhelming relief that washed over me when I realized I was truly safe. But the fire had caused significant damage to my mother's apartment, which was the very first home she had secured on her own. This apartment was her pride, her independence, her sanctuary. Knowing that my actions, however unintentional, had brought destruction and distress into something she had worked so hard to build left me devastated.

And yet, her response was not blame or anger. It was love. She was only concerned that I had made it out alive. Her resilience and grace taught me something I carry with me to this day: the irreplaceable value of life, and the unconditional strength of a mother's love.

This experience was more than a close call; it was a miracle. It taught me about caution, responsibility, and the unseen grace that can guide and protect us even when we are unaware.

"No weapon that is formed against thee shall prosper; and every tongue that shall rise against thee in judgment thou shalt condemn. This is the heritage of the servants of the Lord, and their righteousness is of me, saith the Lord."

— Isaiah 54:17 (KJV)

Say this Prayer of Protection:

Lord, cover me with Your protective wings, shield me from fear, and grant me assurance that Your love surrounds me like a mighty fortress by day and night. And please hold me close and don't let me go. In Jesus' Name, Amen!

Worship Reflection: *"More Than I Can Bear"* – Kirk Franklin

TESTIMONY 3

Happy 13th Birthday to Me: Angels Watching Over Me

Defying Death: How Divine Protection Turned a Near-Fatal Crash into a Miracle of Survival

What began as a day of birthday candles and celebration turned, in a split second, into a fight for my life. On my thirteenth birthday, a day that should have been filled with celebration and joy, I found myself in a life-threatening car accident. While my mother was turning a corner, the power steering suddenly gave out, sending the vehicle crashing into a pole.

The impact was violent. I struck the windshield headfirst, but in that moment, I felt no pain, just shock. I remember the eerie calm that came over me, followed by the slow, terrifying realization as warm blood began to trickle down my face.

At the emergency room, the attending physician quickly assessed the danger: my wound was dangerously close to a major vein near my temple. He explained that operating near that area was far too risky. One wrong move could be fatal. With no other option, he made the decision to stitch the wound closed, without anesthesia. I can still recall the raw intensity of that pain. My aunt would later tell me that the sound of my screams echoed through the halls of the hospital. It was a moment of sheer agony; but it was also a moment of divine intervention.

Afterward, the doctor pulled my family aside and said words I will never forget: "If the impact had been even a fraction of an inch over, she would not be here. She is truly a miracle." That truth hit me harder than the windshield ever could. I had narrowly escaped death. The accident should have taken my life, but somehow, I was still standing. Still breathing. Still alive.

That moment awakened something in me. I knew, with absolute certainty, that it was not luck or coincidence that spared me. It was God. His hand was upon me… guiding the outcome, surrounding me with mercy. And though I didn't fully understand it then, that accident became the spark that ignited a deeper journey of faith and purpose. I had been protected for a reason. My life was preserved for something greater.

"For he shall give his angels charge over thee, to keep thee in all thy ways."

— Psalm 91:11 (KJV)

This verse resonates so personally with me. I truly believe that God commanded His angels to stand watch over me that day. Even when I didn't know I needed saving, He had already sent help.

Worship Reflection: *"Angels Watching Over Me"* – Richard Smallwood & The Group Virtue

Worship Reflection: "*How Much We Can Bear"* – Pastor Hezekiah Walker

TESTIMONY 4

"Grandmother, Is That You Calling Me?"

When the Quiet Voice Breaks Through: Hearing God's Call in the Stillness

There are moments in life that feel ordinary, until suddenly, they're not. Moments when something invisible yet undeniable breaks through the routine and demands your attention. One night, in the quiet of my own home, I experienced such a moment, one that awakened my spirit and stirred something deep within me.

It began while I was in the shower. I distinctly heard my name being called, softly, but clearly. At first, I assumed it was my grandmother. She had a gentle, reassuring way of calling me that I had always trusted. But when I stepped out to check, I found that she hadn't called me at all. No one had. Still, I heard it again.

The experience left me unsettled, the voice echoing in my thoughts and spirit. I couldn't shake the feeling that something deeper was unfolding, something beyond the natural. Later that evening, as I was lying on the couch, an object unexpectedly fell onto my head. The suddenness of it startled me. My first thought was that someone had broken into the house. But after checking and finding nothing out of place, I sat in silence, reflecting on the strange sequence of events.

What had first filled me with fear began to feel like something else entirely, a divine interruption. It was as though God was calling for my attention, gently but persistently, until I finally listened. I now believe that both the voice and the unexpected jolt were not coincidences or accidents. They were moments of spiritual prompting, God's way of saying, "I am here. Listen."

This experience ignited a deeper awareness in me. I began to understand that God doesn't always speak through thunder or lightning; sometimes, He whispers. And if we're too distracted or skeptical, we might miss the call. That night awakened a sense of divine purpose and a renewed commitment to live more attentively, more prayerfully, and more obediently.

"And the Lord came, and stood, and called as at other times, Samuel, Samuel. Then Samuel answered, Speak; for thy servant heareth."

— 1 Samuel 3:10 (KJV)

Like Samuel, I didn't fully recognize God's voice at first. But now, the conviction that He was calling me is undeniable. This moment of divine encounter has taught me the importance of listening, truly listening, when God speaks.

Although I considered myself the "bad" one and often felt like my friends were the "good" ones, God still decided to choose me. He called me, equipped me, and is using me, not because I was perfect, but because He is faithful. I am grateful for the miracle of being chosen. That truth humbles me and reminds me that His grace isn't based on our qualifications, but on His purpose, and our willingness to say yes.

If you've ever felt a similar stirring or heard an internal voice nudging your spirit, I encourage you not to dismiss it. Lean into it. Pray. Listen. Respond. Sometimes, God speaks quietly, but His message is life-changing.

Worship Reflection: *"Speak to My Heart, Lord"* – Pastor Donnie McClurkin

TESTIMONY 5

An Atmosphere Shift: He's Calling Me

From Resistance to Revelation: When Unwanted Change Becomes God's Divine Calling

Change has a way of finding us when we least expect it, and often when we least want it. What feels like disruption at first can later be revealed as divine direction. I came to understand this truth through a personal journey of transition and growth, one that reshaped my life and deepened my faith.

My recent relocation from Cleveland, Ohio, to Elgin, Illinois, was not something I anticipated. It was brought about by a significant change in my family circumstances. As my grandmother grew older, she lovingly explained that she could no longer care for me as she once had. With that, it was decided that I would go to live with my mother.

At first, I was overwhelmed with frustration, confusion, and even resentment. I didn't understand why my life had to be disrupted or why this change had come so suddenly. I struggled to accept that the plans I had for myself were now being replaced by a future I had not chosen.

But as time passed, I began to see with new eyes. What I had first viewed as a setback slowly revealed itself as a setup, a divine repositioning. This move to Elgin, a place that had once been completely unfamiliar to me, began to feel like a fresh start rather than a forced detour. I discovered new opportunities, made meaningful connections, and found strength in the very change I had resisted. What once felt like disruption, I now see as a miracle.

Now, I can look back and recognize that God was moving even when I couldn't see it. This transition, though uncomfortable, was the beginning of a deeper transformation within me. It taught me to trust Him in the unknown, to listen more carefully for His voice, and to believe that even when things feel out of control, God is still in control.

"No man can come to me, except the Father which hath sent me draw him: and I will raise him up at the last day."

— John 6:44 (KJV)

This verse reminds me that nothing in our lives is random; our steps are ordered, and it is God who draws us to where we need to be, often before we understand why. I believe He was calling me, not just to a new city, but to a new season, a new purpose, and a deeper walk with Him.

Worship Reflection: *"He's Calling Me"* – Rev. Frank E. Ray, Sr.

TESTIMONY 6

The Call That Saved & Changed My Life

When Chaos Replaces Calm: Learning to Trust God Amidst Unseen Battles

There are seasons in life when the weight of change feels almost unbearable, when everything familiar is stripped away, and you're forced to navigate an entirely new reality. That's exactly what happened when I moved to Elgin, Illinois. I had no idea that this new chapter would become one of the most difficult seasons I'd ever walk through.

Before the move, I lived in a peaceful home with my grandmother, a sanctuary where quiet nights brought comfort and safety. But once I relocated, everything changed. The home I entered was filled with constant chaos, family members arguing late into the night, the sounds of fighting and unrest replacing the calm I had once known.

I knew my mother and father loved me, but the chaos, laughter, loud music, and arguments that filled their late-night parties were often overwhelming. Many nights were spent wide awake, heart pounding, struggling to find peace in a place that felt so different from the calm of my grandmother's house. And the impact wasn't just emotional, it affected every area of my life, especially school. I struggled to concentrate in class. I often fell asleep during lessons, worn down by stress and exhaustion. The mental and emotional noise followed me everywhere, and I found myself retreating into sleep just to escape it.

Though I had already witnessed God's miraculous protection; surviving a house fire and a serious car accident, I now faced challenges that stretched my faith in new ways. I thank God for my praying grandmothers: Earle Minnette Steel Smith (Gram) and Ollie Mary Beck Johnson (Mae), better known as Grandmother.

I knew nothing about Child Protective Services or where to turn for help, but desperation drove me to seek a way out. One night, after watching a TV program about domestic abuse and the brave individuals who found strength to ask for help, I realized I could no longer endure the turmoil in silence.

With a mixture of fear and hope, I reached out to Child Protective Services. What followed was a quick and caring response. Mr. Copeland, along with others, offered support that gave me much-needed relief and the strength to face the uncertainty ahead.

It wasn't an easy road, but the decision to ask for help became a turning point in my life. Slowly, I began to see glimpses of peace again. And with that peace came the ability to refocus and push through, one day at a time.

"I can do all things through Christ which strengtheneth me."

— Philippians 4:13 (KJV)

That verse became my truth. I wasn't thriving academically, but I was surviving, and that in itself was a miracle. I didn't retain much from elementary or middle school, and for a long time, I struggled with the fear that I wouldn't make it. But God had the final say.

Looking back, I know one thing for sure, it's a miracle that I graduated high school. I truly believe it was by the grace of God that I made it through. He heard my quiet, desperate prayers, and He answered them. What should have been impossible became reality, not because I was strong, but because He was.

"For the gifts and calling of God are without repentance."

— Romans 11:29 (KJV)

This verse reminds me that God's call on my life remains unwavering, even through the hardest trials. Though the road has been tough, I walk forward confident that I am fulfilling the purpose He has set for me.

Worship Reflection: *"He's Calling You"* – Pastor Donnie McClurkin

Worship Reflection: *"I Had a Praying Grandmother"* – Helen Baylor

TESTIMONY 7

Wow! My Last Name is Johnson too!

Divine Placement: How Unexpected Relationships Opened the Door to Spiritual Transformation

Sometimes, God places people in our lives not just to help us for a moment, but to change our direction entirely. That's exactly what happened when I met the Johnson family. What began as a brief foster placement soon opened a new chapter in my life, one filled with warmth, guidance, and a sense of belonging I had longed for.

After a short time back home, I was invited to attend church with Sister Wilma Jean Johnson, whom I affectionately called Mommy. This invitation marked the beginning of a meaningful five-year relationship that deeply shaped my spiritual journey.

The remarkable coincidence of sharing the Johnson surname with my God-given family, combined with my move from Cleveland, Ohio, to Elgin, Illinois, felt like nothing short of a divinely orchestrated miracle. I believe God's hand was clearly at work, placing me exactly where I needed to be.

Under Mommy's loving mentorship, I began to develop a stronger prayer life. She continually stressed the importance of salvation. As I watched her walk with Christ, she made it seem effortless. The time I spent with her was a season of growth and encouragement. She helped nurture the talents God had gifted me. Mommy helped me discover my true calling: to deepen my faith and build a personal, living relationship with Jesus Christ as my Savior.

One night during a revival, I surrendered my life to Christ. I walked to the altar with trembling hands and a desperate heart. I prayed the Sinner's Prayer from *Romans 10:9–10*:

"That if thou shalt confess with thy mouth the Lord Jesus, and shalt believe in thine heart that God hath raised him from the dead, thou shalt be saved. For

with the heart man believeth unto righteousness; and with the mouth confession is made unto salvation."

With tears streaming down my face, I cried out, "Save me, Lord! Save me, Lord!" over and over again. The weight of every sin, every fear, and every failure pressed on my chest as I pleaded for forgiveness. I repented with my whole heart, not holding anything back. My voice broke as I confessed my sins out loud, weeping uncontrollably, hands lifted in surrender.

Then, something shifted in the atmosphere. I felt the Holy Spirit overshadow me, thick, undeniable, and real. A warmth rushed over me, and I began to clap my hands and shout praises. I spoke in tongues as the Spirit gave utterance, just like in Acts 2. My cries turned into rejoicing. Others gathered around me, praying in the Spirit, laying hands on me, and encouraging me to press in. I felt chains break. I felt free.

That night marked the beginning of my true relationship with Jesus, not religion, not routine, but a living, breathing connection with the Savior who met me at the altar and changed my life forever.

"As every man hath received the gift, even so minister the same one to another, as good stewards of the manifold grace of God... If any man speak, let him speak as the oracles of God; if any man minister, let him do it as of the ability which God giveth."

— 1 Peter 4:10–11 (KJV)

Worship Reflection: *"Send Me, Lord"* – Matt Redman

TESTIMONY 8

Curbside Blessing – A Miracle at Hand

Grace in the Unexpected: How God's Timing and Loving Hands Saved My Life

Some experiences stay with you, not just because of what happened, but because of how clearly God shows up through others when we need Him most.

One afternoon, something happened that reminded me just how much we're held, not only by God's grace but also by the care and presence of those around us. And on that day, God sent someone I know and love: Mother Dorothy Richardson.

I was grateful that my job was only a short distance from my house. On this particular day, during my lunch break, I decided to walk home. I made myself a simple meal, a bologna sandwich, some chips, and a soda. After eating, I had just enough time to make it back to work. But as I ran toward my job, I was suddenly struck with a severe and overwhelming illness. The onset was immediate, leaving me disoriented and in excruciating pain. I remember falling onto the curb, clutching my stomach in agony before losing consciousness.

I woke up to the voice of a fellow church member, Mother Dorothy Richardson. Not knowing how long I had been unconscious, her presence at that exact moment felt like a divine appointment, a true blessing from God. Had she not been there to see what happened and respond so quickly, the outcome could have been far worse.

I was hospitalized for a week for tests and observation. Yet, after all the scans and procedures, doctors found nothing. I was released without a diagnosis. It was truly a miracle, a clear sign that God's hand of protection was at work once again.

I am immensely grateful for Mother Richardson's quick thinking, her immediate call for emergency medical assistance quite literally saved my life. This incident has deepened my appreciation for the supportive circle of faith within our church community and reminded me that God's grace often arrives through the hands and hearts of others. Though it was a frightening and unsettling experience, the kindness and care I received that day became a powerful testimony to God's faithfulness. I remain forever thankful to Mother Dorothy Richardson and continue to carry the memory of that moment with gratitude of heart.

"In every thing give thanks: for this is the will of God in Christ Jesus concerning you."

— 1 Thessalonians 5:18 (KJV)

"Thou shalt not be afraid for the terror by night; nor for the arrow that flieth by day."

— Psalm 91:5 (KJV)

Prayer of Protection:

Heavenly Father, I thank You for being my ever-present help in times of trouble. I ask for Your divine protection over my life, shield me from danger seen and unseen. Protect me from the arrows that fly by day and the fears that come by night. Let Your angels be assigned to watch over me wherever I go. Strengthen me with peace, wisdom, and discernment. In Jesus' Name, Amen.

Worship Reflection: *"Show Up!"* – John P. Kee & New Life Community

TESTIMONY 9

Rest for the Weary – Only Rider – Greyhound Bus

When a Prayer for Space Became a Journey of Grace and Unexpected Rest

During my frequent travels between Elgin, Illinois, and Cleveland, Ohio, I experienced a remarkable moment that reaffirmed my faith in God's care for every detail of our lives.

I often found myself on crowded buses. One particular trip, a fellow passenger's constant movement made the ride especially uncomfortable. Wedged tightly between people much larger than me, I felt trapped and overwhelmed. In that moment, I whispered a simple, heartfelt prayer: "Lord, let me be the only rider on the bus."

The week before Christmas, I was waiting at the downtown Chicago bus station when I noticed something unusual: the station was nearly empty. There were far fewer passengers than usual, and my bus, (normally punctual), was delayed.

When I asked the station staff if buses were still departing, they explained there was a shortage of both drivers and riders. The weather was clear, so nothing seemed to explain the stillness. As I stood there thinking to myself, *This is strange…* it hit me: could this be the answer to the prayer I had whispered?

Eventually, a bus driver arrived, one I had never ridden with before. As departure time neared, so did my anxiety. When I asked him about the delay, he confirmed it was due to the low number of passengers. I sat waiting, unsure if we would even depart. Then, in a quiet moment of grace, he invited me to board the bus, as the only passenger.

He smiled and said, "They usually don't let a bus go over the road for just one person, your ticket doesn't even cover the gas." But this time, they made an exception.

What a powerful answer to my prayer.

My relief soon shifted to apprehension as I remembered the prayer I had whispered earlier. Fear tried to creep in, what if this wasn't a blessing, but a setup? I was the only passenger on an empty bus riding with a stranger. My mind raced with doubts, wondering if I had made a mistake.

But then, the driver introduced himself, not just by name, but as a pastor. His gentle tone and kind words immediately offered reassurance. He spoke with a calm authority that brought peace to my spirit.

As the bus rolled onto the road, I quietly meditated on the prayer I had prayed and how God had already answered it. I chose to trust Him. My meditation was interrupted by the driver, who stated that he was my guardian angel and urged me to get some rest. Then the fear began to fade, replaced by a sense of safety. I knew without a doubt, I was protected.

The driver kindly allowed me to rest during the trip, promising to wake me up when we arrived. This simple act gave me the break I desperately needed. I had been balancing work, family, and church commitments, and I was overwhelmed and exhausted. That quiet bus ride, with its unexpected miracle, became a sacred moment of rest and peace.

God cares for us down to the smallest details.

The bus made its usual stops in South Bend, Indiana, and other locations, but no one else boarded. Upon arriving in Ohio, I reflected on the experience. While my initial prayer may have seemed selfish, I was deeply moved by how tenderly and precisely God responded.

This experience strengthened my belief in the power of prayer, and in the quiet, undeniable reality of miracles.

And as our brother in the gospel, Donald Lawrence, reminds us in his song "There Is a King in You," there is power in what we speak, so we must be mindful of the words we release.

"Fear thou not; for I am with thee: be not dismayed; for I am thy God: I will strengthen thee; yea, I will help thee; yea, I will uphold thee with the right hand of my righteousness."

— Isaiah 41:10 (KJV)

"Come unto me, all ye that labour and are heavy laden, and I will give you rest. Take my yoke upon you, and learn of me; for I am meek and lowly in heart: and ye shall find rest unto your souls."

— Matthew 11:28–29 (KJV)

Worship Reflection: *"He Has His Hands on You"* – Pastor Marvin Sapp

TESTIMONY 10

A WARNING! A MESSAGE! – HELL IS REAL!

When the Spirit speaks through dreams, it's time to rise; will you be ready for His return?

My spiritual journey has presented both challenges and triumphs. While I strive to live a life that honors my faith, I've experienced periods of struggle, times when my actions didn't align with my beliefs. I felt a growing distance from God, even though I knew there was a strong calling on my life. That tension between calling and conduct weighed heavily on me.

Then one night, it all came to a head in a powerful, transformative dream. In that dream, God vividly revealed the consequences of my choices. There was no sugar-coating, it was direct, sobering, and clear. It was as if He was warning me personally, showing me what could happen if I continued down the wrong path. The urgency to align my actions with my beliefs became crystal clear. What I experienced at that moment was not just a dream. It was the miracle of God revealing truth and calling me back to Him.

The impact of that dream was so strong, I felt compelled to write immediately. What poured out of me became the play titled *Will You Be Caught Up?* This wasn't just a script, it was a spiritual reckoning, a wake-up call, and a testimony all in one. The speed and clarity with which the play came together felt nothing short of divine. I truly believe it was God-inspired. That experience changed my life and renewed my commitment to live in faith and obedience.

In that season of renewed obedience, God used my mom, Atoy Bray-Spates (Wisdom), in a way that has been a point of reflection and conversation down through the years. The role she has always played in my real life, as a steady, praying, wise mother, showed up so naturally and powerfully on stage. In my stage play, *"Will You Be Caught Up?"*, she didn't just act, she stepped onto the stage exactly as she has always been, that bold, loving mother figure. It wasn't a performance; it was her heart, her spirit, and her lived testimony shining through.

In the opening scene, she ministered Daryl Coley's "He's Preparing Me," and that song set the tone for everything that followed. The message of the song always tugged at my heart; God was preparing me for bigger than I could yet carry shaping me in love and care for what was ahead.

Hearing those words through her melodious voice hit differently because I knew she believed them, and in that moment, I needed the reminder.

"The steps of a good man are ordered by the Lord: and he delighteth in his way. Though he fall, he shall not be utterly cast down: for the Lord upholdeth him with his hand."

— Psalm 37:23–24 (KJV)

"Then we which are alive and remain shall be caught up together with them in the clouds, to meet the Lord in the air: and so shall we ever be with the Lord."

— 1 Thessalonians 4:17 (KJV)

Worship Reflection: *"Will You Be Ready"* – Commissioned

Worship Reflection: *"The Sky Shall Unfold"* – Vickie Winans

Worship Reflection: "Calling My Name"– Hezekiah Walker

TESTIMONY 11

Cinnamon Toast Crunch – My Brown Sugar Miracle

When doors seemed closed, faith opened a way; believe for it, and watch miracles unfold

My journey to motherhood began with a deep desire for a husband and family. I have always wanted to pour the love I received from my mother and grandmother into my children–nurturing, guiding, and cherishing them. Yet, at the time, traditional thinking made it difficult for a single woman to be considered a mother. I was also determined to never have children out of wedlock, which made the path feel even more uncertain. Often, it seemed as though the door to motherhood was closed before I could even knock.

But then things began to shift.

When the regulations changed, allowing single women to become foster parents, it was nothing short of a breakthrough. I saw it as a divine opportunity. Eagerly, I joined the program designed to support single foster parents and waited patiently for a placement, believing that the right child would come in God's perfect timing.

After an extended period of waiting, I received a call asking if I could provide respite care. I said yes without hesitation. That one simple yes changed my life forever.

The child I was entrusted with for that brief time brought instant joy. I affectionately nicknamed her "Cinnamon Brown Sugar," a sweet name that came from a momentary lapse in remembering her real one, but it stuck. The name matched her perfectly: warm, comforting, and full of personality. What began as temporary respite care quickly transitioned into a full foster placement, and that placement blossomed into a five-year journey of love, growth, and healing.

Eventually, by the grace of God, that journey led to adoption. I became a mother, me, a single woman who once thought the doors to motherhood were closed, am now living in a miracle of answered prayer.

Reflecting on it all, I'm filled with awe and gratitude for the divine orchestration that brought my daughter into my life. It was nothing short of miraculous.

"Therefore I say unto you, What things soever ye desire, when ye pray, believe that ye receive them, and ye shall have them."

— Mark 11:24 (KJV)

The song that echoes this testimony in my heart is *"Believe for It,"* CeCe Winans; because I did, and God answered!

TESTIMONY 12

Miss Christian World Pageant 1991 – An Unbelievable Win!

When faith leads the way, God crowns our dreams with purpose and favor

From an early age, I was surrounded by people who nurtured both my faith and my dreams. Among the most influential were my godparents, Elder Leonard Spates Jr. and Sister Kansadie Spates. Their love, encouragement, and unwavering belief in me helped shape the woman I would become. Growing up under their spiritual guidance, alongside the community at Spates Temple Church of God in Christ in Elgin, Illinois, planted the seeds of purpose in my heart.

Long before I ever stood on a stage, I carried within me a quiet but persistent dream: to one day compete in a beauty pageant. That dream was born in Cleveland, Ohio, where, as a little girl, I would sit glued to the television screen, watching pageants with wide-eyed wonder. I wasn't only mesmerized by the gowns or the crowns, it was the grace, confidence, and talent of the contestants that fascinated me. Even then, I wasn't seeking attention for beauty's sake. I wanted a platform to express who I was and what I believed in.

After moving to Elgin, Illinois, the dream didn't fade, it intensified. With the loving support of my godparents and spiritual community, I felt encouraged to pursue it seriously. I eventually confided in Superintendent Leonard Spates Sr., my pastor at Spates Temple COGIC, about my desire to enter a local Miss Black America Pageant. His response was thoughtful and grounded. While he admired my ambition, he voiced concern, particularly about the swimsuit competition, which I, too, had hesitations about.

Pastor Spates Sr. encouraged me to continue seeking a pageant that aligned with my Christian values. He reminded me that it's not only about physical appearance, but about character, intellect, and honoring God through the gifts He's given us.

Unfortunately, I would later learn that the pageant had been discontinued before I had the chance to participate. Even so, I held onto my dream.

Determined to honor God with my pursuit, I began searching for a faith-based pageant, one that would allow me to showcase both my talents and my walk with Christ. My search led to a disheartening truth: Christian-centered pageants were extremely rare.

Then, in what I can only describe as a miraculous moment, God made a way.

One evening, after coming home from work, I was surprised to find the television on, and even more surprised to see it tuned to a channel we rarely ever received airing a commercial for the Miss Christian World Pageant. I couldn't believe what I was seeing. The age requirement was 18 to 25, and I had just turned 25. I still qualified!

There was one more stipulation: contestants could not have children. At the time, I had not yet officially adopted my daughter. While I had been given the green light to proceed, the adoption wasn't finalized, which meant I still met the eligibility criteria.

I auditioned, submitted my application, and was accepted. It was a beautiful moment, one filled with excitement, hope, and a deep sense of divine confirmation. I recall standing in my kitchen when the Holy Spirit spoke clearly to my heart: You will win.

Yet the road to that stage wasn't without its challenges. Some contestants attempted to disqualify me because of my foster daughter. But just as He always has, God stood by me. His favor shielded me, and every weapon formed against me failed. Through every trial, He reminded me: My plans for you are final.

When my name was called as the winner, I didn't feel shocked, I felt affirmed. The Scripture had proven true: "Seek ye first the kingdom of God… and all these things shall be added unto you." The applause, the crown, the recognition, none of it compared to the quiet joy in my heart. I knew this was God's doing.

To this day, my pageant experience remains a powerful testimony of how God honors faith, perseverance, and purity of purpose. With the steadfast love of my godparents, Elder Spates Jr. and Sister Candy Spates; the spiritual leadership of Superintendent Spates Sr.; the unrelenting prayers of my Spates Temple church family; and the love and support of my own family, I was able to walk boldly in my calling. What began as a little girl's dream became a demonstration of God's faithfulness, and proof that when you align your desires with His will, nothing is impossible.

"Favor is deceitful, and beauty is vain: but a woman that feareth the LORD, she shall be praised."

— Proverbs 31:30 (KJV)

"But they that wait upon the LORD shall renew their strength; they shall mount up with wings as eagles; they shall run, and not be weary; and they shall walk, and not faint."

— Isaiah 40:31 (KJV)

Worship Reflection: *"It's My Winning Season"* – Jekalyn Carr

TESTIMONY 13

The Word of Life!

In the midst of pain, God's power spoke; and I am still here by His grace

The power of God through prayer is real, and I experienced it firsthand.

While coming home from work, out of nowhere, I was hit with a headache so painful, so intense, I honestly thought I was going to pass away. The suddenness of it terrified me. The stabbing pains that pierced through my head felt like tiny knives cutting into my brain, intensifying with every heartbeat and making it impossible to focus or think clearly. Moment by moment, my very thoughts were being shattered.

I was overwhelmed with fear and desperation. Fear began to overtake me, and the raging thoughts flooded in, Who would care for my daughter? Would my mother be able to bear the responsibility? I cried out, God, please! Then, I took every negative thought captive and leaned fully on my faith, trusting God for healing.

Then, God answered me in a way I will never forget.

I used what little strength I had to climb the stairs to my apartment. Upon entrance, it was my desire to get to my bed. Due to my loss of strength and pounding head, I only made it to my roommate Jackie's room. Not being able to rest without background noise, I turned on the television attempting to get the gospel channel. I adjusted the antenna trying to get a better signal, something I did often with no success.

Suddenly, a clear picture of Bishop T.D. Jakes appeared on the screen. He began preaching about someone having a headache. His description of the pain mimicked exactly what I was experiencing. Then he prayed, declaring that God had a purpose for those suffering such pain and would not let them perish.

As he prayed, the pain vanished, just like that.

It was an immediate, undeniable healing. I was overwhelmed by God's power and mercy. Looking back, I truly believe I encountered the weight of His glory, a powerful, overwhelming presence that filled the room with peace, awe, and undeniable holiness. It was a powerful reminder that He sees us, hears us, and moves in miraculous ways. That day changed everything for me. It showed me clearly that miracles are real, prayer is powerful, and God's healing touch is alive and active.

If you're struggling today, hold on. Don't lose faith. Miracles still happen, and God is listening.

"I shall not die, but live, and declare the works of the Lord."

— Psalm 118:17 (KJV)

Worship Reflection: *"I'm Still Here by the Grace of God"* – Dorinda Clark-Cole

TESTIMONY 14

A Ray of Sunshine – A Promise Kept

A prayer whispered in grief was answered with the sun's gentle embrace, a sign of heaven's peace

Grief has a way of slowing everything down. It invites you to pause, reflect, and hold tightly to the people and moments that have shaped your life. In the midst of deep sorrow, I found myself remembering not just the loss, but the love, the legacy, and the quiet ways God shows up when our hearts are breaking.

I am still processing the profound loss of my grandmother. She was such a significant figure in my life, a true matriarch who embodied strength, love, and unwavering faith. I have countless childhood memories of sitting at her feet, simply feeling her comforting presence. She was my lifeline, my encourager, my best friend, my mother, and my protector.

My grandmother was a member of Affinity Missionary Baptist Church, located at 4411 East 175th Street in Cleveland, Ohio, a church that nurtured her faith and became a spiritual home for our family over the years. Her dedication to her family paralleled her dedication to building the Kingdom of God. She nurtured us with home-cooked meals, ensured we had a balanced and healthy diet, and instilled in us the importance of faith and family.

One day, while at work, I received a disheartening call from a family member informing me that my grandmother was in the hospital and her condition wasn't looking good. In my anguish, my only concern was that my grandmother make it to heaven. In desperation, I prayed: "God, if You decide to take my grandmother, please let me know she went to heaven. If I recite a poem at her funeral, let the sun shine after I finish." I kept that prayer close to my heart and didn't share it with anyone.

During her hospitalization, it was initially stated that she was unable to communicate. Without asking any questions, my faith rose up, and I was determined to hear her voice. I remember the desperate call to the hospital, demanding that they put my grandmother on the phone. I pleaded for her to respond and prayed for her recovery. With a faint breath, my grandmother whispered, "Hello." I told her that I loved her, and the nurse immediately took the phone, explaining that my grandmother needed her rest.

I later found out that she had contracted spinal meningitis and, unknowingly, ruptured her spleen. In an attempt to soothe the pain, she applied a heating pad. Tragically, the heat caused toxins from the ruptured spleen to spread throughout her body. Despite her strength and what the doctors described as good internal health, the infection ultimately took her life.

The doctors were fascinated by how well-preserved my grandmother was. Her body showed no visible signs of aging. They were amazed that every organ was strong and intact. Internally, she was thriving, a reflection of how well she had cared for herself over the years.

Her passing was devastating.

While I was still in Elgin, Illinois, preparing to travel for her funeral, the weather report from Cleveland was discouraging. A storm was approaching, and it looked like it would be a gloomy day.

On the day of her funeral, just as the forecast had said, a storm had rolled in. It was very gloomy outside. Although sad, I tried to remain focused. As I stared at the rain sliding down the church's stained-glass windows, tears slid down my face. I sat in silence, remembering all the cherished moments my grandmother and I had shared. As I looked around, I couldn't help but smile inside. The church was beautifully decorated. There were flowers everywhere, and I recognized faces I hadn't seen in quite some time. As I absorbed my surroundings, I was comforted by how deeply my grandmother was loved.

When I was called up to recite the poem I had written for her, From A to Z: What You Mean to Me, I felt God's presence. I boldly stood in the pulpit and spoke every word of the poem from beginning to end.

When I finished, I stepped down and laid my head on my grandmother's casket. My face was turned toward one of the stained-glass windows. As I lay there, eyes shut tight, I wept. Then, out of nowhere, I felt the sun's rays beaming on my face. The sun had broken through the clouds and shone into the church, lighting it up like precious jewels sparkling on a necklace.

When we arrived home, my mother said to me, "Rale," (that's my nickname), "when you finished your poem, the sun started to shine."

No one had known about the prayer. Not even my mother. But God did.

It was more than coincidence; it was a miracle confirmed. A quiet, undeniable reminder that God had heard me. Even in grief, His hand was still upon us.

This experience, though wrapped in sorrow, reaffirmed my faith and reminded me of the enduring power of prayer. It is a testimony of profound loss, but also of miraculous grace. My grandmother's life and legacy continue to inspire me, and I carry her memory with me every day.

"And God shall wipe away all tears from their eyes; and there shall be no more death, neither sorrow, nor crying, neither shall there be any more pain: for the former things are passed away."

— Revelation 21:4 (KJV)

Worship Reflection: *"I Shall Wear a Crown"* – Thomas Whitfield

TESTIMONY 15

My Last Call

Covenant Love – Prayer, patience, and trust; God's recipe for a love that lasts a lifetime

For years, I prayed for a husband, earnestly, persistently, and sometimes with tears. Friends would encourage me with kind words, reminding me that "God has someone special for you," but with each passing year, hope began to feel like a fading light. I had loved before, but none of those relationships led to marriage. One by one, they ended, leaving behind questions, disappointment, and eventually... a cross-country move from Elgin, Illinois, to Houston, Texas.

That move turned out to be more than just a relocation, it was a divine setup. It was in Houston that God answered my heartfelt desire and sent me the man who helped to change everything. Not just any man, but one whose heart mirrored Christ's: kind, respectful, devoted, and full of faith.

Before that blessing came, I navigated the wilderness of chat-line dating, and it was not pretty. Too many of the men I engaged in conversation with were chasing convenience, not covenant. Some wanted companionship without commitment; others made promises with no intention of keeping them. I knew what I wanted: a relationship built on godly values, mutual respect, and unwavering love. I refused to compromise.

There were lonely nights and moments of weakness, even times I questioned whether I'd misunderstood God's plan for me. But even in doubt, I clung to faith. I kept praying. I kept believing. When it seemed like the marriage door had closed for good, I made the decision to step away from the search entirely. I resolved that if God wanted me to be married, He'd make it happen, His way, in His time.

Then, it happened.

My now-husband was the final person to contact me through a phone-chat dating service. That last call turned into a conversation that lasted all night. We didn't talk about surface-level things, we talked about life, faith, purpose, and family. He didn't flirt or push boundaries; he listened, he shared, and he respected me. His sincerity caught me off guard in the best way.

Even more remarkable, he was open to starting a family later in life. His patience, character, and unwavering faith made it clear: he was the one I had prayed for.

Twenty years later, I look at our marriage and see the hand of God all over it. We've journeyed through different denominations, from Church of God in Christ to Baptist to non-denominational, but our foundation in Christ has never shifted. Our love isn't just a beautiful story; it's a living, breathing testimony of God's faithfulness.

To every woman still waiting, still praying, still wondering:

Don't give up. Your miracle might be just one unexpected connection away. What God has for you, no one can take. Stay faithful, stay expectant, and trust His timing.

"Whoso findeth a wife findeth a good thing, and obtaineth favour of the Lord."

— Proverbs 18:22 (KJV)

Worship Reflection: *"God Woman"* – Phil & Brenda Nicholas

Worship Reflection: *"A Love Like This"* – Phil & Brenda Nicholas

TESTIMONY 16

The Prayer! The Birth! The Call!

A Journey of Faith, Loss, and Unexpected Blessings

Life took me through valleys I didn't choose, but God led me to the family I always prayed for.

Sometimes life takes you through the darkest valleys before leading you to the brightest blessings.

From the very beginning, I always wanted a family, a son and a daughter, but my journey to motherhood was anything but easy.

I went through a traumatic experience that resulted in an unwanted abortion after a date rape. That time was incredibly painful, and I struggled with it for a long while. Then, I suffered a miscarriage. Those moments broke my heart, but they also drove me closer to God. Prayer became my refuge, my source of strength. I prayed earnestly, surrendering my desire for children to God's perfect will.

During the tough time of family transition, my foster daughters, Mi'Kina and Miaunique, had to leave. Their departure left a hole in my heart. It was hard, really hard. I prayed for their safety and well-being every day, holding onto hope that they'd be okay. That period of loss made me stop and really think about what the future held for my family.

For three days straight, I dedicated myself to deep prayer, asking God to give me clarity and guide my next steps. I left the decision fully in His hands, trusting He would show me the way.

And then, it happened.

Out of nowhere, I got a phone call, a call that offered me the chance to adopt a baby boy. It felt like a miracle. Three days of praying. Three days later, a birth. And three days after that, was the call that changed my life forever.

I became a mother to a precious son, Robert, who is now 18 years old.

This journey has strengthened my faith beyond words. It showed me the power of prayer, forgiveness, and how God's miracles unfold in ways we don't always expect. I share my story hoping it will bring hope to anyone walking through similar challenges.

To those of you still waiting and praying, don't lose heart. God's timing is perfect, and your blessing could be just around the corner.

Now, I just want to say how incredible it feels to have such an amazing family. Maya, Kina, Asia, Trey, Robbie, and Mil, you six bring so much laughter, love, and fresh perspectives into my life every day. It truly brightens my world.

We've definitely had our ups and downs, and I want to take a moment to acknowledge that I haven't always gotten everything right. There were times when things I said, (though meant as loving correction) caused hurt. For that, I am truly sorry. I ask not only for your forgiveness, but also for your grace, as my intentions came from a place of care, even when the delivery wasn't perfect.

Through it all, the love we share has been our steady anchor. It means everything to me. Honestly, I wouldn't trade this wonderfully crazy bunch for anything.

Life gets hectic, and adjusting to all the beautiful chaos hasn't always been easy. But my heart is full, and I'm so deeply grateful for each of you.

"But the God of all grace, who hath called us unto his eternal glory by Christ Jesus, after that ye have suffered a while, make you perfect, stablish, strengthen, settle you."

— 1 Peter 5:10 (KJV)

Worship Reflection: *"Love"* – Kirk Franklin

TESTIMONY 17

One Thousand Twenty-Nine Dollars

Faith, Discernment, and a Purse Full of Miracles. God's grace covered my misstep, and His favor returned what the thief tried to take.

It's amazing how one ordinary decision, simply sticking to your routine, can collide with divine prompting and set the stage for a miracle.

My daughter had just given me her rent money, $1,029. My plan was to immediately deposit it into my bank account, but I figured I had time to stop at the YMCA for a quick workout. Sticking to my fitness routine felt important, and that small choice changed everything.

As I pulled into the parking lot, something in my spirit stirred. I noticed two individuals sitting in a parked car, and a gentle warning rose up in me. Something didn't feel right. But instead of fully leaning into that prompting, I semi-ignored it. I told myself not to be paranoid.

Rather than bringing my purse into the gym with me, I tucked it under my jacket and placed it underneath the driver's seat. After ensuring it was carefully covered, I made sure the doors were locked, then headed inside to begin my workout, still brushing off that inner nudge.

Upon finishing my workout, I was headed to my car when an extremely frantic woman approached me, asking if I had seen anyone near her car while I was walking my outdoor laps. I could barely understand her through her frantic cries. She exclaimed that her car windows were busted and that her laptop and purse had been stolen. Immediately, my heart dropped as I remembered my own purse, with my daughter's rent money, $1,029.

I went full speed to my car. With each step closer, my heartbeat picked up. By the time I reached the vehicle, I was in a full-blown panic. Realizing my windows were not busted gave me a bit of hope, but as I opened my car door, I instantly realized I too had been victimized. The jacket I had used to cover my red purse was now on the passenger seat, with no purse in sight.

I stood there in shock, unable to breathe. The weight of what had just happened hit me like a ton of bricks. I felt sick. I had a full-blown panic attack right there in the YMCA parking lot. I cried repeatedly, out loud, "How will I pay my daughter's rent?! God, please!"

The community of patrons from the YMCA surrounded me. They began to go into their personal pockets and started giving me money. I said that I could not take it, but they insisted that I did. I was humbled but still broken.

This wasn't just about the money. It was the realization that I hadn't listened to the Holy Spirit. I had been warned, and I had ignored it.

After calling the police and filing a report, all I could do was pray and try to steady my heart. But at that moment, I honestly believed the money, and everything else, was lost forever. With tears streaming down my face and my voice completely shattered from sobbing, I called my sister, Nakia. The moment she picked up, I broke down.

I could barely get the words out.

"Nakia… my purse… it's gone… all the money, it's gone. Everything…"

I was inconsolable, choking on sobs as grief and guilt overwhelmed me. I felt like I had failed, failed to listen to the Holy Spirit, failed to protect what was entrusted to me, failed myself.

But Nakia didn't respond with panic. She didn't try to rush through my pain. Instead, she rose up in the Spirit and immediately went to war for me. Her voice came through the phone strong and steady:

"We're going to pray. What do you want God to do?"

Even in the middle of my breakdown, I knew what I desired. Through broken words and trembling breath, I managed to whisper, "I want my purse back, with all the money in it. I want the thieves to have a change of heart. Even if they don't give it back to me directly, let them throw it out the window between the YMCA and the church."

We locked arms in the Spirit, and she prayed out loud, fervent, and full of faith. She called on God with authority, speaking scriptures of restoration, mercy, and divine intervention over the situation. One key prayer point that I remember is that she asked God to blind them from seeing the money. Every word she prayed became a lifeline, pulling me back from the edge of despair. I could barely speak, but in my spirit, I agreed. I believed with everything in me that God could still do something miraculous. Though I couldn't find the strength to pray out loud, I locked arms with Nakia in faith.

And then, the miracle

Not long after, I received a call from the YMCA. They told me someone had recovered my purse. Even more shocking, they were on the way to personally return it to my home.

When the man arrived, I opened the purse with trembling hands, expecting at least some of the money to be missing. But to my absolute disbelief, every single dollar was still there including a slightly torn $100 bill. Nothing had been taken. Nothing was missing.

I tried to offer the man a reward, but he refused it. "Returning it with everything inside was reward enough," he told me.

I was overwhelmed, humbled, grateful, and in awe. I had witnessed a miracle unfold in real time. God didn't just restore what had been stolen; He reminded me of His mercy, even in moments when I ignored His voice. He also reminded me of the goodness that still exists in the world, through the unexpected kindness of strangers.

This experience taught me never to dismiss that still, small voice of the Holy Spirit, because even when we falter, God is able to restore what was lost.

After the man left, I drove directly to the YMCA and returned every dollar that had been given to me. The community of patrons was shocked. They expressed appreciation for my integrity.

If you've ever made a mistake and thought it was too late for God to step in, hear this: it's not. His grace covers even our missteps, and His power can still turn everything around.

"And the Lord turned the captivity of Job, when he prayed for his friends: also the Lord gave Job twice as much as he had before."

— Job 42:10 (KJV)

Worship Reflection: *"Turning Around for Me"* – VaShawn Mitchell

Worship Reflection: *"Worship Adonai"* – Lisa Bracy

TESTIMONY 18

Top of the Line!

Storms, Setbacks, and the Power of Advocacy

Sometimes the storm doesn't just knock out the lights; it exposes deeper battles that need to be fought with both faith and courage.

After a severe storm hit the Houston area, many were left struggling, including myself. The storm caused severe power outages, resulting in entire food supplies spoiling. Seeking help, I turned to our local agency for emergency assistance. I wasn't alone. Five of my friends, all African American and from different zip codes, were also in need of the same urgent support.

To our surprise and confusion, all five of us were denied aid.

The decision felt like more than just a bureaucratic hurdle; it pointed to something deeper. The disparity was too clear to ignore, and something within me knew I couldn't stay silent.

Hoping for a miracle, I contacted the agency directly, not to argue, but to ask honest, necessary questions: How were these funds being allocated? What criteria were they using to determine who received support? Was race or zip code influencing decisions? I requested transparency, a demographic breakdown of who had received aid so far, including race, ethnicity, and area.

I knew the conversation might make some people uncomfortable. But I also knew it was necessary.

Shortly after my inquiry, I received confirmation: a grant would be given to me.

I don't believe that outcome was coincidence. It was the result of persistent advocacy, paired with prayer, faith, and boldness. God gave me the strength to speak up, not just for myself, but for others who felt voiceless. This wasn't just about getting assistance. It was about standing in the gap and trusting God to bring justice where it was lacking.

This experience reminded me that favor is real, and often, it flows when faith and action walk hand in hand.

So, to anyone feeling overlooked, mistreated, or dismissed: Speak up. Pray. Ask questions. Advocate for fairness. And above all, trust that God sees it all. Your voice matters. And with Him, breakthroughs are always possible.

"So shalt thou find favour and good understanding in the sight of God and man."

— Proverbs 3:4 (KJV)

Worship Reflection: *"F.A.V.O.R."* – Kirk Franklin

Worship Reflection: *"Show Up"* – John P. Kee and The New Life Community Choir

TESTIMONY 19

Grace Granted – Southwest Airlines

A Dream Job, A Difficult Decision, an Unshakeable Faith

Sometimes the door you've waited so long to walk through opens to reveal a path you didn't expect to take.

When I was offered a position at Southwest Airlines, I felt a burst of excitement and gratitude. It was a dream opportunity. At a time when the company had limited openings, I was chosen. That alone was a miracle blessing. Even passing their series of tests with a 92% during the loss of my grandson, Jaxon, was a miracle as my mind was not in the space to retain information.

The job turned out to be everything I'd hoped for and more. The culture was inspiring, the leadership supportive, and the benefits outstanding. It felt like I had found the perfect fit, professionally and personally. Every part of the experience affirmed that I was exactly where I was meant to be.

But life has a way of shifting our plans.

Due to unforeseen family circumstances, I had to make the incredibly difficult decision to step away from my position. It was heartbreaking. Walking away from something so aligned with my goals and values wasn't easy. But at that moment, I knew my priorities had to be redirected.

Though my time at Southwest Airlines was brief, it left a lasting mark on my heart. It strengthened my resolve, affirmed my career direction, and deepened my admiration for a company that truly values its people. Even in leaving, I felt blessed, because the experience itself was a gift.

And that's what I hold on to: the blessing.

This journey reminded me that success isn't always measured by how long something lasts, but by what it deposits in you while it's there. Faith taught me to release what I couldn't control and trust that God's plan is always greater, even when the timing doesn't make sense.

During training at Southwest, one phrase stood out to me and stayed with me far beyond the job itself:

"Show yourself some grace."

It became more than a slogan; it became a personal reminder to be patient with myself, especially in seasons of change and letting go.

So, to anyone feeling discouraged by unexpected detours, I say to you: Don't forget God; His grace is sufficient for you. Stay hopeful. What feels like an ending may just be a redirection. Keep moving forward, knowing that what God has for you can't be taken, only rerouted in His perfect time. And most importantly, show yourself some grace.

"Now the God of hope fill you with all joy and peace in believing, that ye may abound in hope, through the power of the Holy Ghost."

— Romans 15:13 (KJV)

Worship Reflection: *"I Believe"* – Pastor Marvin Sapp

This song reminded me to keep believing, even when things didn't unfold the way I expected. It carried me through disappointment and helped anchor my hope in God's bigger picture.

TESTIMONY 20

From Pain to Peace: A Mother's Redemption and a Daughter's Prayer

Some miracles unfold quietly, through years of struggle, moments of repentance, and the gentle grace of God at life's end.

Throughout my life, I've witnessed God's hand in powerful and personal ways. From the spiritual transformation of loved ones to the quiet strength He gave me through deep loss, my journey has been marked by both hardship and incredible grace.

One of the most sobering miracles I've experienced came through my mother, Shirley Ann Johnson-Smith. Her life was not an easy one. She battled addiction, faced devastating loss, and endured severe illness. But even with everything stacked against her, my mother carried a beautiful spirit and a gift for cooking that brought joy to so many.

Eventually, life brought her to Houston. By then, she had lost her husband, George Christopher Smith III. Her health was declining, and her heart was heavy with regret. Yet even in this brokenness, I saw God's love pursuing her. I had the opportunity to share the love of Christ with her, and she received it. She renewed her faith, joined a church, and began a journey of spiritual healing that brought me unspeakable joy.

Her transformation was nothing short of miraculous.

As her health continued to decline, she faced another enormous challenge: the removal of her vocal cords. She could no longer speak, yet even in silence, her faith spoke volumes. When the time came for her final days, my heart cried out to God. I prayed that He would not let her suffer, that He would allow her to pass peacefully, gently, and without pain.

There's one moment I'll never forget. I had arranged for a nurse to come and sit with my mother so that her granddaughter, Milla, who had become her primary caregiver, could go out to celebrate her birthday. Later, I called and canceled the nurse, thinking it was no longer needed. But the nurse showed up anyway.

And when she arrived, she immediately noticed something was wrong. She gently told me, "Your mother is dying."

In that moment, I was overcome. I turned to God in urgent prayer, pleading with Him not to take my mother on Milla's birthday. I didn't want that day of celebration to be forever marked by grief. I begged God for just one more day.

And God answered.

My mother went home to be with the Lord the next day, November 21st. He honored my plea, and in doing so, gifted us peace even in the midst of sorrow.

Hallelujah! God did it!

Her passing was not filled with pain, but with peace. And even in that, I saw the hand of God.

This experience deepened my faith like nothing else. It reminded me that God sees the whole picture. He redeems. He restores. And when we call on Him, He hears us.

I share this testimony so that others might be encouraged to believe for the seemingly impossible. No matter your past, no matter your present, God's love reaches deeper. His miracles are real. And when we place our faith in Him, we can find peace even in our most painful moments.

"And this is the confidence that we have in him, that, if we ask any thing according to his will, he heareth us: And if we know that he hear us, whatsoever we ask, we know that we have the petitions that we desired of him."

— 1 John 5:14–15 (KJV)

This worship anthem captures the heart of surrender and the miracle of being fully seen and used by God, despite our pain, our past, or our doubts:

"Here I Am" – Pastor Marvin Sapp

TESTIMONY 21

Just One Sip!

*Healing in the Midst of Crisis: A Testament to Faith and Family**

The doctors called it a miracle, but I call it the power of prayer and the hand of God! I walked out without oxygen, but not without praise!

— God healed me!

When I was diagnosed with severe COVID-19 pneumonia, the odds were stacked against me. Doctors were honest: my condition was critical, and my chances of recovery looked slim.

From the start, the symptoms were overwhelming. As I lay there weak, and in pain, struggling for every shallow breath, even with oxygen, intense fear crept in. With each announced code blue echoing through the halls, I became more and more uncertain of my own outcome. I had no choice but to lean into prayer, not just for myself, but for those in rooms and hospital beds scattered throughout the hospital hallways. Silently, I prayed for families: for children, parents, grandparents, aunts, and uncles. For brothers and sisters. For all loved ones. I prayed that supernatural healing would take place.

I hate to admit it, but it was a dark and frightening time.

When the time came for me to be released from the hospital, the doctor said words I'll never forget:

"It's a miracle. You're blessed to be going home without oxygen."

Those words confirmed what I already knew in my heart: God had healed me.

Even though I was discharged, I was still very weak. My appetite was gone, and my sense of smell had not returned. The only thing I could do was rest. My children were helpful, encouraging, and uplifting during my time of sickness, doing what they could to support me. My husband Ricky, though sick with COVID himself, put his own pain aside and became the strength for both of us. Every day, he gently encouraged me, saying, "Just try to eat something..." But nothing seemed to help.

Then, one day, my sister Nakia brought over a pot of homemade soup. She called to say she had left it at the front door. That simple act of love made all the difference. It was the only thing I could eat, and for the first time in days, I could actually taste something.

That soup nourished me and helped me begin regaining strength. To this day, my sister laughs every time I recount this miracle.

Nakia's care, Ricky's support, and God's grace all came together in that moment, and from there, my healing continued. I am forever grateful for their compassion and for the miraculous way God worked in my life.

Throughout this journey, prayer and faith were my anchor.

I share this testimony to encourage anyone facing hardship: hold on to hope. No matter the struggle, God's healing and restoration are real and available.

"Heal me, O Lord, and I shall be healed; save me, and I shall be saved: for thou art my praise."

— Jeremiah 17:14 (KJV)

"For I will restore health unto thee, and I will heal thee of thy wounds, saith the Lord."

— Jeremiah 30:17 (KJV)

"For I know the thoughts that I think toward you, saith the Lord, thoughts of peace, and not of evil, to give you an expected end."

— Jeremiah 29:11 (KJV)

These songs perfectly echo my heart and journey, expressing thankfulness for healing and grace:

"I Wanted to Say Thank You" – Lisa Page Brooks

"God Is a Good God" – Lisa Page Brooks

"Grateful" – Pastor Hezekiah Walker

"There Is a Miracle in This Room" – Tasha Cobbs Leonard

Now that you have read these testimonies, take a moment to reflect. Miracles are not always grand or dramatic events. Sometimes they are found in the quiet ways God shows up in our lives: protection we didn't see coming, doors that opened at just the right time, strength when we felt weak, or help that arrived when we needed it most. Many of us have experienced miracles without even realizing it in the moment.

Think back over your own life. What miracle has God already done for you?

Write it down.

____

____

____

____

____

____

____

____

____

____

____

REFLECTION TIME

Miracles come in many forms, sometimes grand and unmistakable, other times quiet and deeply personal.

In this collection of 21 miracle testimonies, you've seen how God's hand moves uniquely in different situations. These stories may not always fit the textbook definition of miracles, but they reveal something far more powerful: the undeniable presence of God's grace, love, and guidance in both the everyday and the extraordinary.

Take a moment to reflect on your own journey with these questions:

Can I now look back and identify moments in my life that may very well have been miraculous, but that I dismissed as coincidence?

How have my struggles and changes led to unexpected blessings or growth?

Am I open to God's quiet whispers, trusting that His voice may come in the stillness or the storm?

Do I embrace the gifts and purposes God has given me, using them to serve others with humility and love?

When life feels chaotic or uncertain, do I seek God's peace and trust His plan even when the path is unclear?

Am I willing to step forward in faith, believing that God's miracles are woven through every chapter of my story?

And most importantly, am I ready for Jesus' return?

Remember, a miracle is not always a moment of spectacle; it is often the gentle unfolding of God's perfect plan: the quiet rescue, the unseen strength, and the unshakable hope that carries us through.

Let these reflections inspire you to see your life as a miracle in progress shaped by grace and empowered by faith.

ACCOMPLISHMENTS

Every step of my journey has been guided by God's hand, often in ways I didn't recognize at the time. Looking back now, I can clearly see how He opened doors, nurtured my gifts, and allowed purpose to unfold through creativity, service, and unexpected moments of recognition. My heart is filled with gratitude for every opportunity, every lesson, and every reminder that obedience and faith never go unnoticed.

As I reflect on my career journey and the incredible opportunities I've been blessed to experience, my heart is filled with gratitude. My path has been richly rewarding, filled with creativity, service, and moments of recognition I never expected, yet deeply cherish.

Over the years, I've had the privilege of performing in theatrical productions and writing a variety of skits that inspired and entertained. One of the most memorable was titled *"Sunday School, Sunday School… Yuck!"*, a fun, relatable piece that still makes people laugh and think. It remains one of my proudest creations.

In addition to the stage, I have been blessed with opportunities in media and ministry communications. I served as a gospel radio host on RHEMA Gospel Radio in Houston, Texas, where I hosted "The Ride Home with RO Show." I am also the host of the YouTube series *The Living Room: Real People, Real Talk*– a platform dedicated to authentic conversations, encouragement, and faith-filled dialogue.

Along the way, I've also received several honors:

- Outstanding Woman of America
- Miss Sunday School
- Recognition from Chicago's First Jurisdiction Choir Department
- The Dr. Martin Luther King Jr. Award from the City of Elgin
- Participation in the Elgin, Illinois Summer Youth Program

Each moment has reminded me of God's grace and the power of using my gifts to serve others.

And this is just the beginning!

Thank you for walking through these pages with me. May the reflections in this book stir your heart, strengthen your faith, and inspire you to walk boldly in your own purpose.

Please stay tuned for the *21 MIRACLE Testimonies* book tour and the launch of an exciting new project: *Chazzie Jazzie Goes to Sunday School.*

Chazzie Jazzie Goes to Sunday School is a heartwarming story that invites children to experience the joy and excitement of Sunday School.

LET'S RETURN TO THE OLD LANDMARK

There was a time when testimony service was the heartbeat of so many churches. It was a sacred moment set aside for believers to stand and declare the goodness of God.

I remember Friday nights carrying a special kind of expectancy. People gathered with hearts full, waiting for the opportunity to share what God had done in their lives. One after another, they would jump out of their seats, overflowing with joy, gratitude, and holy excitement to testify about answered prayers, breakthroughs on their jobs, healing in their bodies, provision in their homes, restored relationships, and unexpected blessings through neighbors, friends, and even strangers.

Somewhere along the way, many churches quietly moved away from the beauty of testimony service. Some pastors, (and even congregants), began to lose interest; saying that the testimony portion of the service became too long, expressing that some did not know when to "cut it off", or, that what should have been a testimony sometimes sounded more like a complaint. Yet, what I remember is something far deeper: I saw excited church mothers, young people, single parents, married couples, etc. people who had waited all week long, eager to pour out their hearts and publicly honor the greatness of our God.

I believe it is time for us to return to the old landmark; those sacred spaces where there is room for everyone to testify, rejoice, weep, and witness the goodness of God together.

The Word reminds us:

"And they overcame him by the blood of the Lamb, and by the word of their testimony..."
— Revelation 12:11 (KJV)

It is my heart's desire to help revive the essence of testimony service by creating sacred spaces where shining light on God's greatness is welcomed, encouraged, and celebrated.

I believe testimonies do more than tell a story; they awaken faith in others. They remind us that if God moved for a neighbor, a friend, or someone sitting in the same room, He is more than able to move in our lives as well.

What may seem small to one person may be life-changing to another, and every testimony deserves room to breathe.

My prayer is that every testimony gathering leaves hearts encouraged, faith strengthened, and hope renewed.

NOW BOOKING LIVE TESTIMONY & STORYTELLING EXPERIENCES

Now booking live testimony gatherings and storytelling experiences for:

- Women's conferences
- Church revival nights
- Women's ministry retreats
- Small group gatherings
- Home fellowship circles
- Prayer gatherings
- Healing and restoration events
- Community faith events
- Special church services

These gatherings can be hosted in churches, homes, retreat spaces, community venues, or intimate small-group settings.

Whether hosted as a women's conference experience, a church revival night, or a small group in the comfort of your home, these gatherings create room for healing, encouragement, breakthrough, and the sharing of God's goodness.

As host, you simply provide the space, and together we create an atmosphere where faith, testimony, and hope can flourish.

Speaking and Booking Inquiries

Email: Info@weshallproductionsent.com
Phone: 888-240-9195

FOLLOW ME ON SOCIAL MEDIA

Facebook: We Shall Productions Entertainment
Instagram: we_shall_productions
YouTube: We Shall Productions Entertainment
TikTok: We Shall Productions Entertainment
Website: www.weshallproductionsent.com

SUPPORT THE MISSION

If this collection of lived experiences, miracles, and faith-filled reflections has touched your heart, your support helps continue the mission of inspiring children, uplifting communities, and creating spaces for healing, hope, and encouragement.

Your support helps fund future testimony gatherings, children's initiatives, community outreach, and faith-based projects rooted in the principle of "each one, teach one."

Every gift helps us create more spaces where testimonies, healing, and hope can live on.

Support gifts may be sent via Zelle:
Weshall2010@yahoo.com

ABOUT THE BOOK COVER DESIGNER

Dr. Denise Wilkins is a visionary creative, acclaimed playwright, author, branding strategist, youth empowerment advocate, and publishing design professional whose excellence and eye for presentation helped bring *21 Miracle Testimonies* to life.

A gifted storyteller with a passion for inspiring transformation through the arts, Dr. Denise has used her voice and creative brilliance to empower communities, uplift youth, and illuminate faith through powerful stage productions and literary works. Among her renowned stage plays is *Black Lights Shining in the Darkness*, a compelling work that reflects the power of God's love, truth, and healing.

Her creative passion can be seen in this project. From concept to cover, Dr. Denise's commitment to excellence helped ensure that this book was presented with the beauty, professionalism, and depth it deserves.

To connect with Dr. Denise Wilkins for book cover design, branding, publishing support, playwright services, youth empowerment initiatives, and creative consulting, follow and connect using the platforms below:

Facebook: Denise Speaks
LinkedIn: Dr. Denise Wilkins
Website: info@justinldavisfoundation.org

Thank you, Dr. Denise, for helping transform this vision into a polished, powerful, and purpose-filled finished work.

ABOUT THE EDITOR

Nakia Dorsey is the visionary founder of *I AM-It's A Movement.* A purpose-driven platform born from lived experiences, and the unwavering passion to help others rise.

Her life journey, marked by both pain and purpose, has given her a deep ability to connect with the broken, the overlooked, and those who feel unseen, unheard, or unable to advocate for themselves. Through years of IDD advocacy, HCS case management, trauma-informed support, and healing-centered service, Nakia's calling remains rooted in one simple promise:

"I will be your voice."

That promise is the heartbeat behind everything she does.

As the editorial visionary behind the formatting, structure, and reader experience of *21 Miracle Testimonies*, Nakia helped preserve the author's authentic voice while ensuring the testimonies were presented with clarity, excellence, and emotional integrity.

Through her brand I AM-It's A Movement, her work reaches communities through outreach initiatives, inspirational speaking, and the unwavering gift of bringing vision to life, no matter the obstacle.

Coming soon: *The I AM Empowerment Mobile.* bringing support, compassion, healing, and hope directly into your community.

To connect with Nakia Dorsey:

Facebook: Nakia Dorsey
TikTok: iam.itsamovement
Instagram: i_am_its_a_movement

Email: ndorsey1999@gmail.com
Phone: 630-675-2624

Thank you for allowing this work to be part of a message that will continue to empower lives for generations to come.

SENDING YOU FORWARD WITH FAITH

If you've read these pages and found a piece of your story reflected in mine; if you've wept, rejoiced, remembered, or felt renewed, know that none of this was by accident. God led you here for a reason.

You are living proof that miracles are still happening. They are found in our healing, in our restoration, in our courage to keep going, and in the quiet, unseen ways God shows up when we least expect it.

Whether your miracle is unfolding now, already behind you, or still on the horizon, keep believing. Keep trusting. Keep praying. Your story isn't over; it is still being written by the One who knows the end from the beginning.

As you close this book, I trust that you are inspired to walk forward with greater faith, deeper peace, and renewed hope. Stay watchful. Stay ready, for Jesus is soon to return.

Thank you for taking this journey with me.

With love, gratitude, and prayer,

Rochelle Johnson-Wiggins

"And God is able to bless you abundantly, so that in all things at all times, having all that you need, you will abound in every good work."

— 2 Corinthians 9:8 (KJV)

"The LORD bless thee, and keep thee: The LORD make his face shine upon thee, and be gracious unto thee: The LORD lift up his countenance upon thee, and give thee peace."

— Numbers 6:24–26 (KJV)

www.ingramcontent.com/pod-product-compliance
Lightning Source LLC
LaVergne TN
LVHW010942110826
845149LV00013B/2727